THE WHOLE WORLD KNOWS MARILYN MONROE.
A FANTASY...
A SYMBOL...
he seven y
A LEGEND...
TRES SEXY...
OUI, WE LOVE MARILYN.
SHE WAS A DREAM...

BUT SHE WASN'T JUST A DREAM...SHE WAS REAL
ULYSSES
HER ACTING TEACHER LEE STASBERG SAID SHE WAS...
IMPULSIVE AND SHY.
STRASBERG
STUDIO MOGUL DARRYL ZANUCK SAID...
NOBODY DISCOVERED HER; SHE EARNED HER OWN WAY TO STARDOM.
THIRD HUBBY ARTHUR MILLER SAID...
SHE WAS A POET ON A STREET CORNER TRYING TO RECITE TO A CROWD PULLING AT HER CLOTHES...

IN HER VERY LAST INTERVIEW MARILYN SAID...
PLEASE DON'T MAKE ME A JOKE.
IT'S NICE TO BE INCLUDED IN PEOPLE'S FANTASIES...
...BUT YOU ALSO HAVE TO BE ACCEPTED FOR YOUR OWN SAKE...

MARILYN WAS BORN *NORMA JEANE MORTENSON* ON JUNE 1, 1926.
A *GEMINI* – LIKE LOTS OF ACTORS...
MAYBE IT'S THE DUAL PERSONALITY TRAIT.
WE LOVE TO ENTERTAIN...
BEFORE THIS THOUGH...HER MOM GLADYS MONROE BAKER HAD A FAMILY.
GLADYS AND JACK BAKER DIVORCED.
HE TOOK THE KIDS.
THEN GLADYS WED EDWARD MORTENSON.

BUT EDWARD TOOK OFF TOO...
THEN SHE MET C. STANLEY GIFFORD...
THAT'S WHERE NORMA JEANE COMES IN...
I HAVE LOUSY LUCK WITH MEN.
EVEN NORMA JEANE'S BIRTH CERTIFICATE WAS MAKE BELIEVE.
TO HIDE THAT SHE WAS BORN OUT OF WEDLOCK.
Official Birth Certificate
city hospital
On this June 1st 1926
Norma Jeane Gifford
Norma Jeane Baker
Norma Jeane Mortenson
Weighing 7 lbs 2 oz

BEING A SINGLE WORKING MOM IS TOUGH.
12 DAY OLD NORMA JEANE WENT TO A FOSTER FAMILY – THE BOLLANDERS.
I'LL VISIT...
NORMA JEANE WAS SHUTTLED BETWEEN FOSTER HOMES AND ORPHANAGES.
SOME FANTASY, HUH?

VALENTINO
GRETA GAR
JEAN HARLOW
NORMA JEANE ESCAPED INTO THE MOVIES.
ABANDONMENT, SEXUAL ABUSE, POVERTY...
JEAN HARLOW
HOLLYWOOD WAS JUST A DREAM.
NORMA JEANE STRING BEAN! NORMA JEANE THE HUMAN BEAN!
HER CLOTHES SEPARATED HER A LITTLE BIT FROM THE REST OF THE GIRLS.

AROUND 1937 SHE MOVED IN WITH KIND "AUNT" ANA.
SHE WAS GOOD TO ME. I FELT LOVED.
CIRCUMSTANCES CHANGED AND AUNT ANA COULDN'T TAKE CARE OF HER ANYMORE.
IT WAS EITHER ANOTHER ORPHANAGE...
HOME FOR WAYWORD YOUTH
I CAN'T BEAR THE THOUGHT!

OR MARRIAGE...
SHE GOT HITCHED TO LOCAL BOY JIM DOUGHERTY.
HE WAS A MERCHANT MARINE. SHE WAS 16.
CALM DOWN SILLY! SIXTEEN WASN'T SO UNUSUAL IN THOSE DAYS.
AND IT BEAT AN ORPHANAGE.
JIM SAID SHE LIKED TO MIX CARROTS AND PEAS BECAUSE OF THE COLORS.
SHE MIXED CARROTS AND PEAS?
WHO KNOWS - THAT'S WHAT HE SAID

DOUGHERTY GOT SHIPPED OFF SO SHE LOOKED FOR WARTIME WORK.
RADIO PLANE
NORM
I SPRAYED BANANA OIL AND GLUE ONTO FUSELAGES.
VERY GLAMOROUS.
SHE DIDN'T SPRAY BANANA OIL FOR LONG...
SHE SIGNED WITH THE BLUE BOOK MODELING AGENCY.
GREAT! BEAUTIFUL, DOLLFACE!

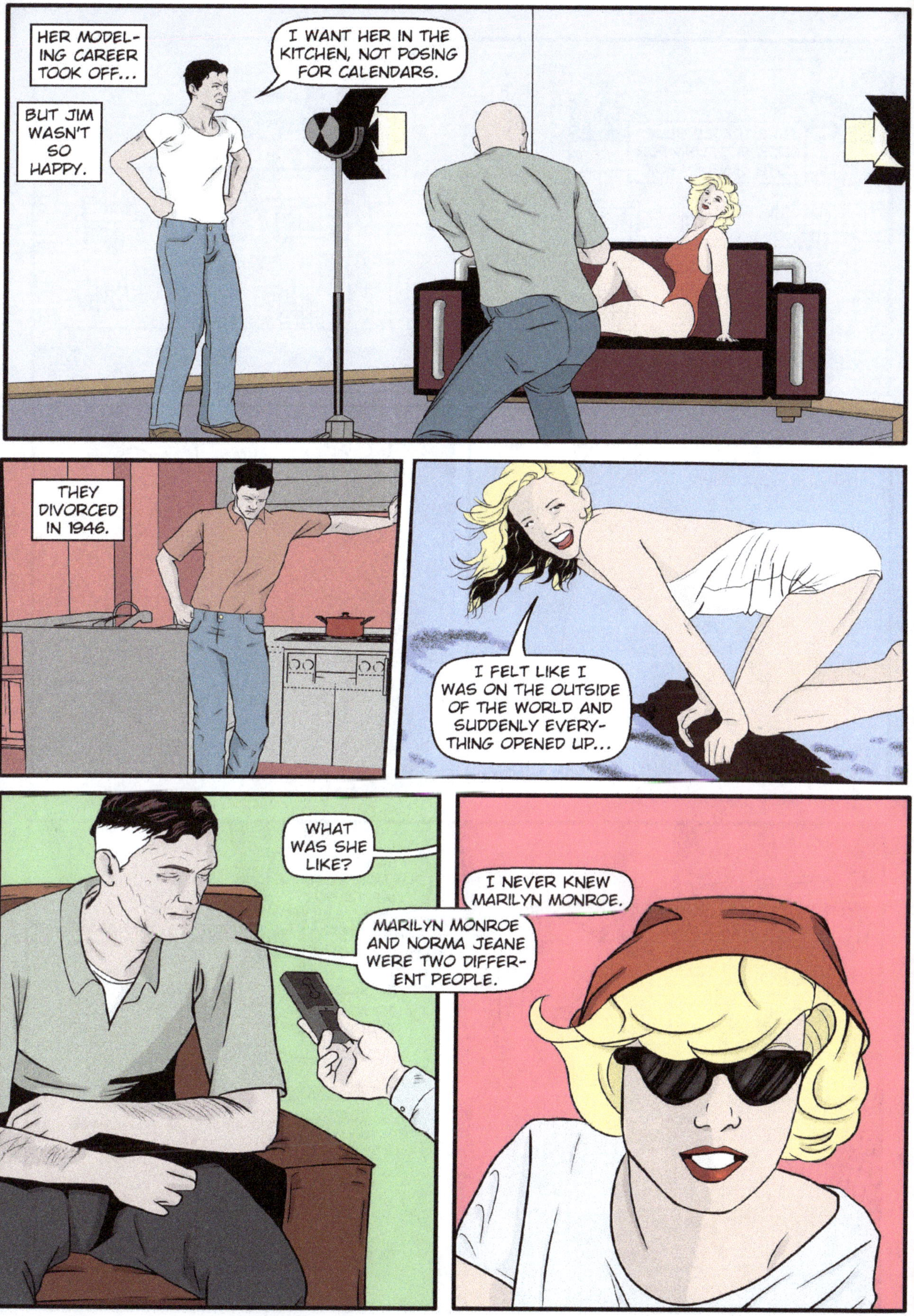
HER MODELING CAREER TOOK OFF...
BUT JIM WASN'T SO HAPPY.
I WANT HER IN THE KITCHEN, NOT POSING FOR CALENDARS.
THEY DIVORCED IN 1946.
I FELT LIKE I WAS ON THE OUTSIDE OF THE WORLD AND SUDDENLY EVERYTHING OPENED UP...
WHAT WAS SHE LIKE?
MARILYN MONROE AND NORMA JEANE WERE TWO DIFFERENT PEOPLE.
I NEVER KNEW MARILYN MONROE.

SHE TRADED BLUE BOOK MODELING FOR 20TH CENTURY FOX.
20th century fox
WE MUST DO SOMETHING WITH THESE EYEBROWS!
MUCH BETTER!
OH MY...
GORGEOUS! BUT NORMA JEANE HAS TO GO...
BUT, THAT'S MY NAME.
DO YOU WANT TO ACT OR NOT DOLL?
YES!

MONROE IS MY MOTHER'S MAIDEN NAME...
BY GEORGE THAT'S IT!
MARILYN MONROE!
MARILYN. MONROE.
MARILYN MONROE!

MY FIRST PICTURE WAS SCUDDA HOO! SCUDDA HAY!
I HAD ONE WORD: "HELLO." IT GOT CUT.
SHE HAD A WALK ON PART WITH GROUCHO MARX.
IS THERE ANYTHING I CAN DO FOR YOU? WHAT A RIDICULOUS STATEMENT...
MR GRUNION, I WANT YOU TO HELP ME...
SHE SHARED A HOLLY-WOOD APARTMENT WITH SHELLEY WINTERS.
THINGS'LL GET BETTER.
I JUST WANT A REAL PART...

WHO'S SHELLEY WINTERS?
OOF! ARE YOU STUPID! LOLITA, A PLACE IN THE SUN, NIGHT OF THE HUNTER... NANA MARY ON ROSEANNE!
OUI! OKAY! VERY TALENTED.
MARILYN AND SHELLEY ONCE GOT DRUNK WITH WELSH POET DYLAN THOMAS
"DO NOT GO GENTLE INTO THAT GOOD NIGHT!"
OOOOH I LOVE THAT ONE MR. THOMAS!
I'M LATE TO GO MEET CHAPLIN!
DYLAN THOMAS CRASHED HIS CAR INTO CHAPLIN'S TENNIS COURT THAT NIGHT.
OOPS...
WE NEED REAL PARTS...
ZZZZZZZZ...

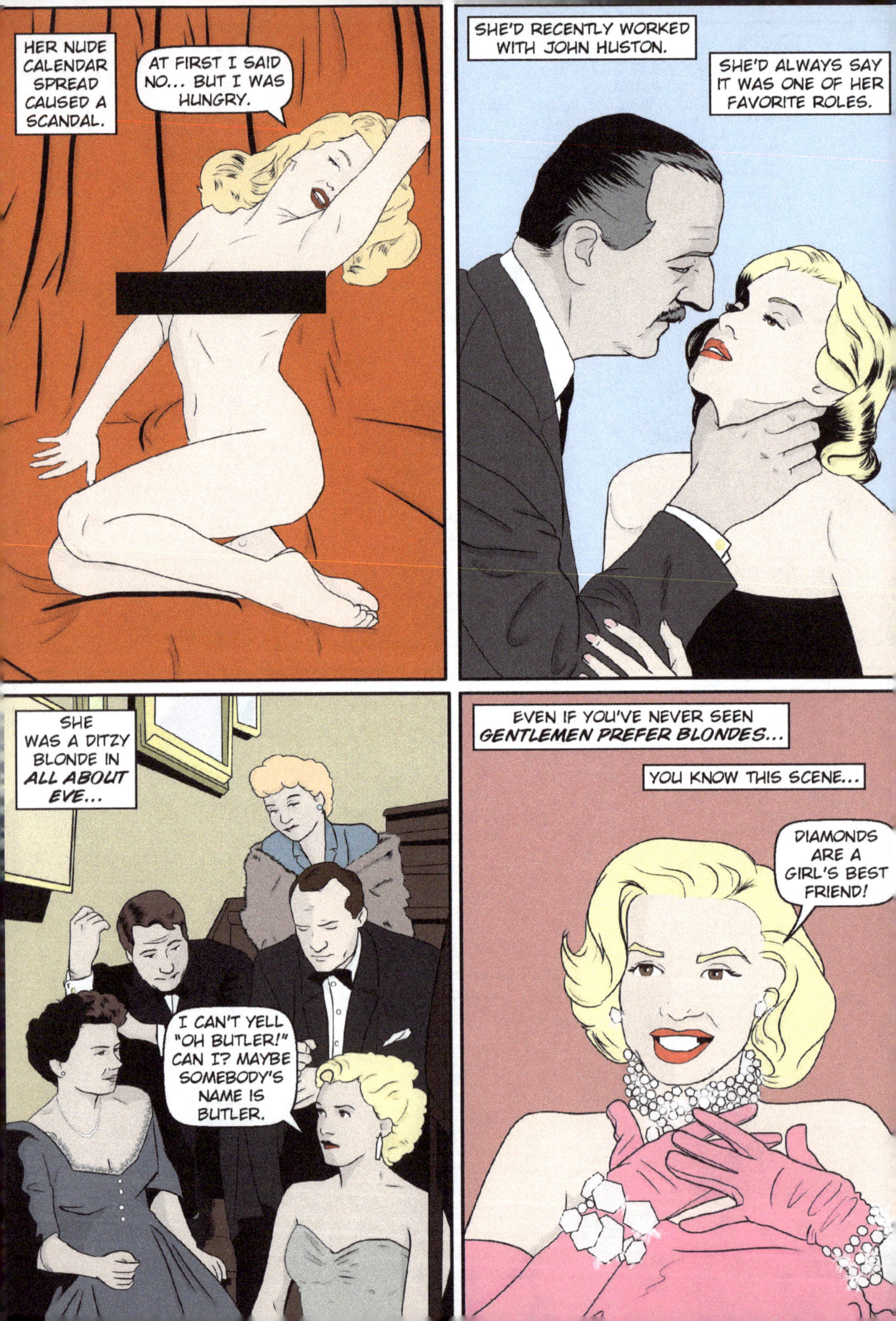
HER NUDE CALENDAR SPREAD CAUSED A SCANDAL.
AT FIRST I SAID NO... BUT I WAS HUNGRY.
SHE'D RECENTLY WORKED WITH JOHN HUSTON.
SHE'D ALWAYS SAY IT WAS ONE OF HER FAVORITE ROLES.
SHE WAS A DITZY BLONDE IN ***ALL ABOUT EVE***...
I CAN'T YELL "OH BUTLER!" CAN I? MAYBE SOMEBODY'S NAME IS BUTLER.
EVEN IF YOU'VE NEVER SEEN ***GENTLEMEN PREFER BLONDES***...
YOU KNOW THIS SCENE...
DIAMONDS ARE A GIRL'S BEST FRIEND!

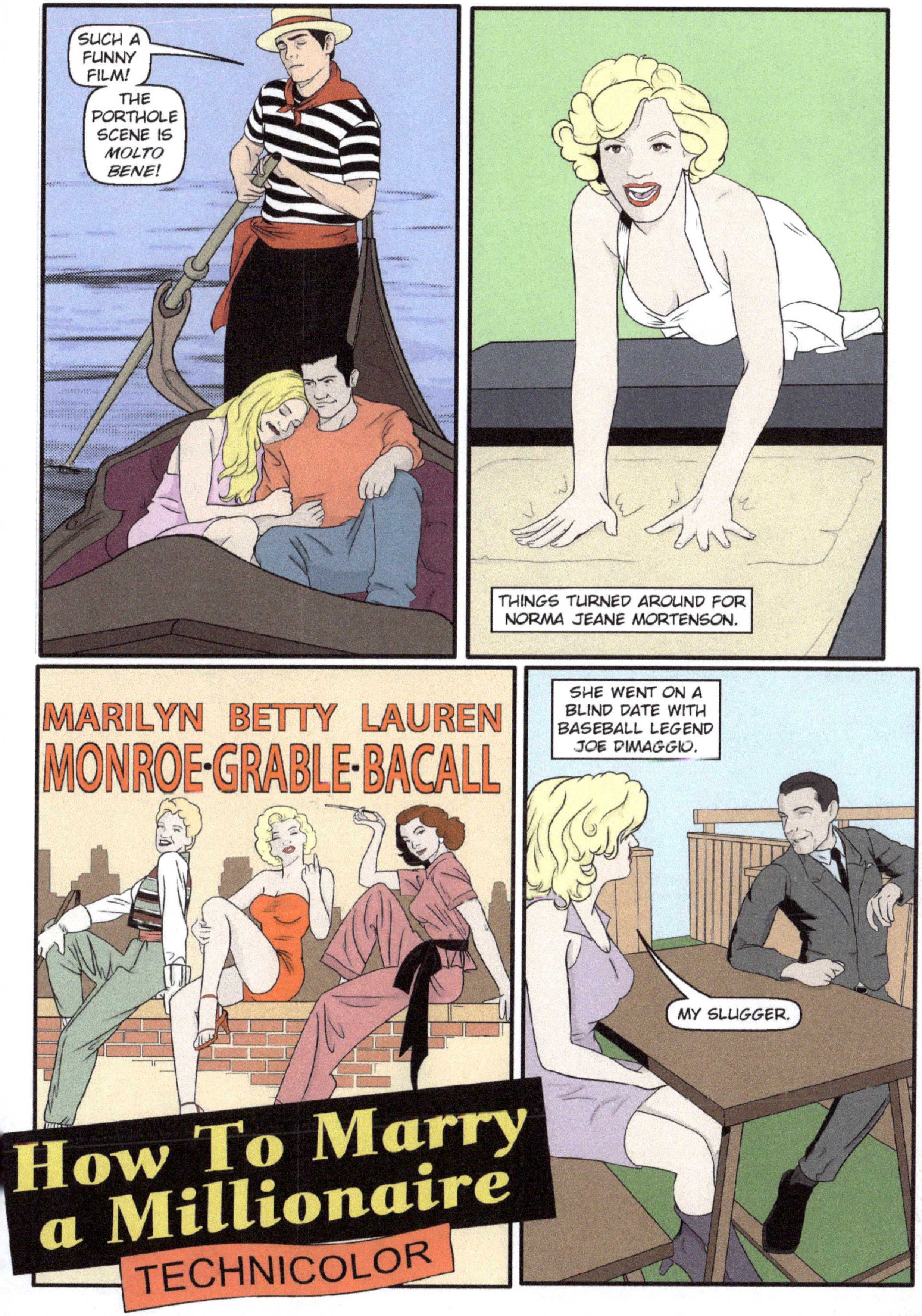
SUCH A FUNNY FILM!
THE PORTHOLE SCENE IS MOLTO BENE!
THINGS TURNED AROUND FOR NORMA JEANE MORTENSON.
MARILYN BETTY LAUREN
MONROE-GRABLE-BACALL
How To Marry a Millionaire
TECHNICOLOR
SHE WENT ON A BLIND DATE WITH BASEBALL LEGEND JOE DIMAGGIO.
MY SLUGGER.

THE MOVIE STAR AND THE AMERICAN HERO.
NOW I CAN HAVE A NORMAL LIFE, A FAMILY...
1950S MARITAL BLISS...
BUT STIRRING SPAGHETTI SOON LOST ITS CHARM.
I GET TO WORK WITH THE GREAT BILLY WILDER!
I DON'T KNOW WHY YOU CAN'T JUST STAY HOME...
NOW I'M GOING TO TAKE YOU IN MY ARMS AND KISS YOU...
Director
lly Wilder

JEWELRY • HATS
COSTUME JEWELRY
ACTION!
JEWELRY • HATS
COSTUME JEWELRY
ISN'T THAT JUST DEEE-LICIOUS!?
YOU GOTTA BE KIDDING ME.
WE LOVE YOU MARILYN!
MARRY ME MARILYN!

YOU'RE MY WIFE!
IT WAS FOR THE FANS - I'D BE NOTHING WITHOUT THEM!

THEY DIVORCED AFTER NINE MONTHS.

...A CONFLICT OF CAREERS...

IT WAS A HARD TIME...

SHE WENT TO SING FOR THE TROOPS IN KOREA.
IT WAS FREEZING OUT, BUT SHE DIDN'T MIND.
DIAMONDS ARE A GIRL'S BEST FRIEND!
IT WAS THE FIRST TIME I EVER FELT LIKE I REALLY HAD AN EFFECT ON PEOPLE.

MARILYN HEADED EAST, TO STUDY WITH THE GREAT ACTING TEACHER LEE STRASBERG.
SHE ALWAYS USED THE SAME PSEUDONYM...
I'M *ZELDA ZONK.*
ZONK?
THAT'S RIGHT. *ZONK.*
THE ACTORS STUDIO
EVEN THOUGH SHE WAS AN INTERNATIONAL STAR, MARILYN CRAVED RESPECT.
THE ACTORS STUDIO
IF I SAY I WANT TO BE AN ACTRESS, THEY LOOK AT MY FIGURE...

SHE ALWAYS SAT IN THE SAME SEAT.
TOWARD THE BACK.
MARLON, YOU DO THE SCENE!
OH...ALRIGHT.
IT'S JUST SO HARD FOR ME TO BE ON TIME.
WELL BE EARLY THEN!
SHE FORMED A PRODUCTION COMPANY WITH FRIEND MILTON GREENE.
NOW I CAN FIND BETTER PARTS.
MAYBE WE CAN BRING MARLON IN TOO.
Ms. Monroe

I HATE YA AND I DESPISE YA!
BUS STOP PROVED TO BE ONE OF HER MOST ACCOMPLISHED ROLES.
I FINALLY FELT RESPECTED.
TIME
AMERICA'S MOST RESPECT-ED PLAYWRIGHT PROPOSED.
SKEPTICS CALLED MARILYN AND ARTHUR MILLER "THE OWN AND THE PUSSYCAT"
I DON'T CARE, I'M IN LOVE.
ME TOO...

NORMA JEANE HAD COME A LONG WAY.
SHE LOVED TO READ.
HER FAVORITE PICTURES WERE THE ONES OF HER WITH A BOOK...
SHE MET FAMOUS WRITERS LIKE CARL SANDBURG, ISAK DINESEN, CARSON MCCULLERS...
THE FOG ROLES IN ON LITTLE CAT FEET!
SHE WANTED A BABY.
BUT IT WASN'T TO BE...

MARILYN AND ARTHUR TRAVELED TO ENGLAND.
I'M THRILLED TO BE WORKING WITH YOU MR. OLIVIER!
THEN BE ON TIME!
HER MARRIAGE WASN'T HAPPY; SHE'D SUFFERED MISCARRIAGES.
MARILYN WAS SLIPPING.
I JUST CAN'T DO IT...
IT'S NOT TOO MUCH FUN TO KNOW YOURSELF TOO WELL...
SHE LIVED IN FEAR OF WINDING UP IN A MENTAL HOSPITAL LIKE HER MOM AND GRANDMOM.

SHE TEAMED WITH BILLY WILDER AGAIN ON ***SOME LIKE IT HOT.***
DON'T FIGHT IT... RELAAAAAAX....
BILLY WILDER SAID HE DESERVED THE PURPLE HEART AFTER WORKING WITH MARILYN.
BUT MARILYN FORGED AHEAD.
THANK YOU!

SHE RE-TEAMED WITH JOHN HUSTON FOR THE MISFITS.
BUT HER MARRIAGE WAS A MESS.
I HAD WOR-SHIPPED CLARK GABLE SINCE I WAS A LITTLE GIRL...
Clark Gable Marilyn Monroe Montgomery Clift
IT WAS THE LAST FILM SHE'D EVER COMPLETE.
Misfits
By: Arthur Miller
SMILE FOR US MARILYN!
WHY ARE YOU DIVORCING ARTHUR MILLER?
WERE THERE AFFAIRS?
YOU'RE NOBODY!
WE LOVE YOU!
DID YOU HEAR ABOUT CLARK GABLE'S DEATH?!

Payne W
Psychiatric
st 61st Stre
I WANTED TO BE AN ARTIST, NOT AN EROTIC FREAK.
DIMAGIO CAME AND GOT HER OUT.
THEY SPENT SOME TIME IN FLORIDA.
YOU'RE GONNA BE FINE.
HER PSYCHIATRIST URGED HER TO BUY HER FIRST HOME.
YOU THINK SO? JUST SOMETHING SMALL...

West Reality
SOLD
THE TILES ADORNING THE THRESHOLD OF HER NEW HOME SAID CURSUM PERFICIO
"YOUR JOURNEY IS OVER" IN LATIN.
CURSUM PERFICIO
SHE JUMPED BACK INTO WORK WITH SOMETHING'S GOT TO GIVE.
IF YOU MISS ONE MORE DAY ON SET YOU'RE FIRED!
SHE DID MISS MORE DAYS.
LIKE WHEN SHE FLEW TO SING TO JFK.
HAPPY BIRTHDAY... MR. PRE-SI-DENT...
SHE WAS A STAR.
BUT SHE COULDN'T SHAKE HER PAST...

MARILYN MONROE WAS FOUND DEAD ON AUGUST 5, 1962.
SHE WAS 36.
THERE ARE MANY CONSPIRACY THEORIES ABOUT HER DEATH.
BUT THAT'S NOT FOR US TO DISCUSS...
OUI, YOU CAN GOOGLE THAT GARBAGE.
THIS IS MY MOST FAVORITE PHOTO.
CECIL BEATON SNAPPED IT.
IT'S HER OWN WEIRD GENIUS THAT HAS SUSTAINED HER FLIGHT...
SHE IS ONLY 15 YEARS OLD AND SHE WILL NEVER DIE.

BLUEWATER COMICS

Dina Gachman — Writer

Nathan Girten — Penciler

Dan Barnes — Colorist

David Hopkins — Letterer

Rob Aragon — Cover

Darren G. Davis
Publisher

Warren Montgomery
Production

Kailey Marsh
Entertainment Manager

Maggie Jessup
Publicity

TIDALWAVE PRODUCTIONS

www.bluewaterprod.com

CPSIA information can be obtained
at www.ICGtesting.com
Printed in the USA
BVHW011721260321
603512BV00007B/792

9 781948 216760